Happy 18th Bday!
I love You so much!

Noni

D1058255

Life *Is* Tough...
but So *Are* You

Copyright © 2018 by Heather Stillufsen.

All rights reserved. No part of this publication may be reproduced, stored in a retrieval system or transmitted in any form or by any means, electronic, mechanical, photocopying, recording or otherwise, without the written permission of the publisher.

ISBN: 978-1-68088-257-5

◖ and Blue Mountain Press are registered in U.S. Patent and Trademark Office. Certain trademarks are used under license.

Printed in China.
Third Printing: 2021

⊕ This book is printed on recycled paper.

This book is printed on paper that has been specially produced to be acid free (neutral pH) and contains no groundwood or unbleached pulp. It conforms with the requirements of the American National Standards Institute, Inc., so as to ensure that this book will last and be enjoyed by future generations.

Blue Mountain Arts, Inc.
P.O. Box 4549, Boulder, Colorado 80306

Life *Is* Tough...
but So *Are* You

Written and Illustrated by
Heather Stillufsen

Blue Mountain Press™
Boulder, Colorado

There will be *times*
when you just
have to take a
deep breath, relax,
and let things *go*.
Focus on *what*
and *who* matter to you.
The rest *will* work
itself out.

Trust your own *heart*...
no one knows
what you want in life
better than you.

What happened
has *happened.*
It's *over*
and behind you.
Don't let the *past*
hold you back.

Sometimes,
what you thought
would be, *isn't*...
but what's going to be
is *better*...

…and sometimes,
what may *seem*
like the end…
is only the *beginning*.

You are in *control*
of where you
are headed.
If things *aren't*
going as planned,
it may be time
to *change* direction!

It's *never* too late
to start over.
Fresh *starts* and
new *beginnings* are
what this life is made of.

At times, you will
be met with obstacles,
but *always* know you
are *capable*
of great things.

When you
start to *doubt*
where it is you are going…
take a moment
to think about
how far
you have come.

Let nothing be stronger than your *determination.* Whatever you are going through is only helping you to *grow* into the person *you* are meant to be.

There are so many *people* in your life who believe in you, support you, and *love* you for who *you* are.

You are *resilient*.
You can overcome
any challenges you
may be facing.
Learn from your mistakes.
Keep a *positive* outlook,
and know that
sometimes *setbacks*
are a part of *success*.

Put fear behind you,
and walk with *courage*
in all that you do.

Keep *hope* with you
wherever you go.
Let it *guide* you through
even the *longest*
and darkest days.

Every *storm*
has a rainbow…
you just have to
look for it.

There will be days when
you feel like giving up,
but don't...
days when you
feel like you just don't
have what it takes,
but you do...
days when everything
seems to be falling apart,
but it won't!

Life is full
of *ups* and *downs,*
but hang in there…
good things
are coming your way.

Remember,
life is *tough*…
but so are *you*.

About the Author

Heather Stillufsen is an artist and writer who fell in love with drawing as a child and has been holding a pencil ever since. Best known for her delicate and whimsical illustration style, her work is instantly recognizable. From friendship to family to fashion, Heather's

Photo by Christine E. Allen

art demonstrates a contemporary sensibility for people of all ages. Her words are written from the heart and offer those who read them the hope of a brighter day and inspiration to live life to the fullest.

Heather is the author and illustrator of four books: *Sisters Make Life More Beautiful, Mothers and Daughters Are Connected by the Heart, May Your Holidays Be Merry and Bright*, and *Life Is Tough… but So Are You.*

In addition to her books, Heather's refreshing and elegant illustrations can be found on greeting cards, calendars, journals, planners, art prints, hand-painted needlepoint canvases, and more.

She currently lives in New Jersey with her husband, two daughters, and a chocolate Lab.